JOKER

JOKER

ARLO HASKELL

SAND PAPER PRESS
KEY WEST

"Then The Stars" and "In The Light" first appeared, in different form,
in *the secret of salt*.

The author wishes to thank Harry Mathews, Marie Chaix, and Bill Wright
for supporting the writing of this book.

ISBN 978-0-9843312-1-5

This book was designed by David Janik in Los Angeles, California. The
typeface is Monotype Scotch Roman, based upon fonts first cut by
Englishman Richard Austin and cast by the Scottish typefounder
Alexander Wilson and Son in Glasgow in the early 1800s.
The edition of 500 is printed on acid-free paper
by McNaughton & Gunn in the
United States of America.

Published by
Sand Paper Press
716 Love Lane
Key West, FL
33040

www.sandpaperpress.net

CONTENTS

for Ashley

Lucky Ducking

The shadows are long, the moon's
not yet set, and the cactus
flowers are puckered open
still like lips which beckon
and expect to taste and feel.

The bigger birds
are singing. Summer's
trying to roll me
and this island.
It's doing the leer,
the weave-and-wobble,
we're doing the flat-
footed-drunk-ducking-punches,
and the aggressors on the
dance floor are the seas
that would surmount us.

Until the rest of these days go by,
there's fear. That's fine. This
day has the usual objects
traversing the regular sky and so–
we can almost count on it–
will the next.

Spearfisher

Mile Zero's hero's
girlfriend's trailing
a ribbon of blood
from her shoulder
as she descends
toward the reef
and his eyes
are on the sky
the Space Shuttle
is leaving.

At the promise
of clear water
I trim the workday short.
I don wetsuit
and fire weapon,
and at impact ascend
to wait for the snapper's
dying to end
from the surface
where I float
satellite-sentry,
catching breath.

The city hems
pedestrian freedoms.
Scripts and lucid code
govern the dazzle
of artificial intelligence,
and our conflated pursuit
is bequeathed by books.

Trouble flees on beats
listeners hear as hope,
adepts or pragmatists
as thoughtless occasion
to glove the tether
and handle the spear,
kicking the quarry home.

Maintenance Man

At the beach and at the store,
the wind is from the south.
It's summer, April,
and fifteen states are under freeze.

I live in the capital island city
of the archipelago where I was born.
The water seems sometimes to rise
like walls armored with slippery scales,
and the lone bridge which plots escape
to another island and another bridge
is like the baitfish retreating
to the boat where it was safe
and where its doom is hatched.

The nearshore waters are as polluted
here as anywhere. The cruise ships
each day thrust silty plumes
that drape the run-down reef.
This insult is my experience;
my charge to mark each day
with tactical kindness, first
considering the options:
to choose to greet the day
with generosity or with selfishness,
with honesty, fidelity, and faithfulness,
or with deceit.

Our Hero's Pastoral

The fellas
on deck
at the after-
party water-
front bar
keep fear in me.

I'm behind
the seagrape
tree, she's behind
those doors,
I can feel it
as I ride around
the block,
eyes out
for flowers to
adorn the spokes
and basket
of her bike,
but summer's
storms have stripped
the trees where
bark bore blossoms
bare, where
cactus blooms reached
out under the moon.

To the florist
tomorrow
I'll go and sit
in the walk-in

refrigerator
where fragrant,
florid winter's come.

His Emergency

I fell off
my bike
last night
riding home
drunk, high:
I
caught a Croton
in the handlebars
and tumbled, tangled
in branches
and bike-frame,
to the sidewalk.

At the hospital
I learned it was a
common bone
to break. I dreamed
of having sex
with the fattest
girl in the fifth
grade, of holding
my infant wife,
of our newborn mouse
trapped in a cooler
full of fresh vegetables.

The Safety

I pick the broken
egg-fruit from the street
and eat it.
Coffee-burned tongue
and I and today's
news are one. Do men
love all these
deaths brought on
by wars, or what?
The long one's escalating
again and every belligerent body
can be blamed. What the fuck
is easy to gasp from the safety
of this lucky accidental country.

Mister October

The secret of
winning lies
in capitalizing
on ungloved mistakes,
plus catching all
the lucky breaks
the pitcher tosses.

A line drive lands
where they're not.
The first baseman
bobbles the ball.

I swing the bat: that's all
it takes. Quick and lasting
wealth and fame clap hands
and trot across the plate.

Then The Stars

Today,
like others: salmon,
sausage, sex, a laptop
afternoon and evening's
entertainment: drinks,
more food, a play,
more drinks
filling the hours
before the week's
collision.

It's easy
to suppose endings
at sunset
but then the stars
are out and
sometimes the moon.
I'll give that drink
back, steer away
from the collision,
make my employer an offer
on his little empire.

The effects of light
and shade at dusk,
redundant, mauve
sky and black almond
leaves before the rats
and raccoons begin
to rustle, are enough.

Autobiography By Puppeteer

1. *Premature Burial*

Date and coconut
and silver palms
peopled the marl, I
held the craft
from the mangrove
bank's shallows.
Crowned pigeons plucked
plums and poisonwood
berries men at rest
shouldn't swallow.

2. *Reinforcements*

I'm pre-occupied
with prosperity.
The lands, canals,
and bays around me
belong to the wealthy.
In time, my currency will grow
blubbery and spill over
the waistband
of the lady garnering
my wages, devouring
me as the sea will
the land, her
boyfriend the last
leaf of garnish.
I mow her lawn

and her daughters' lawns,
and sup on the taste
the teller's take
leaves on my fingers.

3. Flame Manipulator

I am observed riding my bike
past an old girlfriend's
parents' house twice each day,
before and after work.

I never build up the courage to try anything.

As kids, we built big bonfires:
tack together a frame of boards,
fill it up with branches,
add a gallon of gasoline,
the match, and watch it go.

4. The Reliable Guardian

My dad was home
when I'd get home
sometimes,
outside the garage
with the co-workers I saw
as major men, his friends:

"Someday we'll have a new game to watch,
without balls, uniforms, helmets, nets, referees, gloves, or pads.
It'll be us on the Jumbotron, unguarded and reliable,
kissing and helping ourselves
to all the beer and toothpaste we can use."

I learned the ceremony's sequence
as a kid: sit, stand, kneel, eat, repeat;
not much to it, really,
until I followed the strings
pulling my eyes to the ceiling
where God's hands were
a small flock of pigeons
fluttering in the pipes' drafts.

Joker

A carpenter in the service
of an inheritor is easily lulled
by the wealth on loan.
A bartender's dream
is the precise execution
of talent, her stage
the expensive room.
For the retail salesperson,
discount and opportunity
herald having already overcome.

At the edge of town, they
consider privilege beneath them,
while challenge is the strong suit
of the joker, self-deception
through mimicry his aim.

Here is my plain face:
my neighbor's dog
is digging a hole
in the dirt to wash off his bath.
This gag gathers laughter.

In the final scene, when sea fog
retreats from blanketing the chain,
it doesn't travel far. It sits just north
in the gulf, where fishermen
punch no clocks and see
sky and sea as one
as they paradoxically ply
the obvious edge.

A Clear Night

Fifty degrees Farenheit's
too cold for playing Texas
Hold 'Em with Simon
and the boys in the carport.
I start down, go up big,
fall down again,
gamble, and lose all
the money I came with.
At home I have Ashley's
hot pumpkin soup and love.
This, that, the moon between
the quiet almond leaves,
and the open oven heating
the little garden apartment we share
grant more than what card players call the river,
or what others know as "the road," "sea," or "plan b."

Beneath The Bleachers

Tonight's
the holiday
party I fear
the least: folks
of my own age,
and big bowls
of hot bourbon
to breathe from.
Some dirty
jokes get made,
innuendos arise
regarding husbands
and wives
and friends,
and love
goes home
in hands
held with lust
in mind.

Santa's Workshop

The season's
nearly washed
over us.
My mom's
consumed with stress
for due reason
and us kids
could care
less, more, what's
family for
if not to
make love
feel like a burden?
My atheist
in-laws
are in town
and Georgia,
too. Drink
will get us
through this one
and kill us.

Liberation Front

The commute
across the lawn
reveals a dispute
among neighbors
and laborers:
hammers and saws
rupturing rightful sleep.

Creeping from rhyme
is as pleasurable as gravel
crunching underfoot
in the lane, or a clear sky
whose lights are strewn
as casually and dustily as gravel.

A taxi-driven couple
along a dirt road
in a recently war-torn
spring vacation destination
sees a pig hung up to bleed out,
a man digging a grave
in the front yard, a toddler
swinging in the hammock
by his sister's hand, and
a crowd gathered at an intersection
around one suddenly coffined,
his bicycle bent but not irreparable.

The laborers are secure in the safety
provided their staccato rhythms
by the code, and the neighbors

have their pool, beneath whose surface
lies a lungful of peace and quiet.
Safety and security are submarine
watchwords, a mantra building bubbles
that seep into the surface air they breathe.

Floodplain

This unease will pass.
The clouds outside
build shade from sun.
Goods fill the market.
A glass of water
suffices for joy, joy
suffices for wealth
given shape as shelter
from weather
at beach-homes.
Rain unfolds from ruin.
Rain runs over
the flowered hills
and brings nearshore
waters into bloom.
Expressions of ordinary
mouths falter at the gates
where guards and the night
prove the strength
of the majority.

A man is dying in his bed, his family near.
Beyond his room's glass is a reach
of the city: a green hill, red and green
baseball diamonds, black-bridged
grayish river leading to the invisible sea.
We're reading short stories.
Some are funny, *Gimpel*
the Fool, some as sad as this:

"The building
is falling apart,"

he says from sleep.
"We can put it
back together," he says.
Goodbye, Saul.

Hello.

Sails, boom, mast, hull.
A thunderclap announces
a lull in the breeze:
the only trouble
for sailors, whose clip
crawls and stops as the rain
falls, breaking congestion
and playing jester for the rest of us,
bringing out the sun. If our ears
could open to what's beyond
the glass, the wind would bring
what governing people say,
"Not today, not tomorrow, but the next,"
with the hot ash from burning trash and dust.

In luxury, we trust.
On Saturdays, an omelette
with tea and the paper.
I oil the gears of my
outdated implement
and plan trips to sea or the beach
to float or watch it all float by:
Rooftop, Chair, Family Portrait, and T.V.
bob along on what's become
–the water's risen–
all sea. We talk. And
neighbors, drifting in the current's take,
wonder, Who will it be?

Politicians dressed as rescuers motor up and say:
"Choose chance carefully.
Promises yield prospects,"
and other nonsense,
the distance between our floodplain
and Olympia being clear:
"The choice is ours," they say.

I'd rather have the tale of Daniel I made up.
The lions aren't hungry.
My brothers' boots are fireproof.
Wickedness will fall.

The horizon's broken now but by the peaks of sails puffing in
fresh wind.
In a lightening rain, the sun, sails, and speakers slip freely off
the record.

This morning,
I wake up early,
that's nothing special;
take a quick dip
in the pool
after yoga,
that's nothing
special too.
When I return
from lunch
(I try to keep away),
the workmen
have begun.
The new roof
they're applying
affords them a view
of the cemetery,

only dead girls
to whistle at,
and so their words
are of their tools
and measurements.

Hell Or

It’s very windy today
–it almost rained–
and I’m walking around town
after work. Those graves
could be cozy
to nap upon, hold feet
from high water.

Handsome-fleshed Heroes Are Hard To Find

The rough-hewn
tongue-and-groove
ceiling planks
suggest us.

Mahogany blossoms
dust the porch
as a wasp pesters.

I'm nectarless.

The pool's cool.

The ceiling fans
keep time from heat.

Our leading lady's
on leave
from suffering.

The Workday Will Never Be The Same Again

Looking back, there was
never a Joker in the deck.
It was stacked with face cards:
extra Queens and extra Jacks.

Friends multiply and friends divide
by lust for facet and task.
So lapidary accretions obscure quarrymen,
so their machines succumb to floods
rendering sunken cities of the everyday,
so their families inherit redaction.

The habit of watching
for the Joker is a borrowing,
an appropriation of talents for cheer.
In this two-dimensional tableau
the facets are pushed flat
and the seam opens up
with force applied until the face
or self begins to drift apart.

A twenty-years struggle
in the bush. Then morning
again, except it's met with emergent
nodes of communication as urgent
as new green hands of bananas.
The believers add it up to a world
where a town's mourning
is immediate as a siren.

Before the breeze lifted
and a bird flew, a call to duty

crackled over the air, each
of three guaranteed echoes
a line in his delinquent epitaph.

Our Hero Among The Stars

(Third Song of Our Hero)

I'm not sure
I agreed
to this
particular
sublimation.
Here I am
in my best
among peers:
handsomely paid
to turn pages
and serve
at my rival's
pianist-provided party.
Have another drink
, sir?

At The Water's Edge

Jack and I
on subtropical winter's
early summer days
fish for cobia
in not-so-deep
but distant
green or blue
gulf waters.
Brought in green,
we brain them
above their dog-like eyes
with a baseball bat;
we hear the brain-case crack.
We move around the deck
and lift their slippery deadweight
into the tall gray cooler's
blood-red ice-water.

Before all that
we look for bait.
The ball they make
is a shadow built
of uncountable flecks
of light that swells,
shimmers, shudders,
dissolves and reappears
like a flock of plovers
and pipers, or starlings,
or a grocery bag and its shadow
in the wind between buildings.

As it rides the currents so
do I, and then there's my
other, pool-side on a chaise
in the shade, contemplating
some birds bathe
and tug the mirrored
branch and sky
until the water's
surface breaks like branches
reach away from trunk
and its heavy whole
lifts and atomizes
becoming something
seen-through and seen.

Seal Of The City

Here at the new settlement
myth is what we work for.
Blue is the color we wear
and yellow is the water in the well.

Imagination is our hard respite
and the birds in the trees are one of a kind: loneliness.

Our law, like love and lust, is liquid,
penned and implemented by impulse.

Our punishment is invisible– unless
you are one of those who hold up
after reading it a page to the light,
studying its perforations and what resemble
in opacity the mackerel-clouds so foreign
to our climate. In that case
it is merely transparent in relation
to the cinder-block walls that keep
and protect the light and joyous moments
of the inventor of our decline.

Downturn

From shore to shining
lawn, plenitude erupts.
Summer's august habitat
culls vacation mindsets,
calmed enough to witness
the vapors condense,
in falling, into a dew
whose droplets magnify
the smallest of single
instances: a blade drawn
against the proffered neck
that last week ritualized
self-defense against
fashionable barbarism.

Over dale, a boat bobs
at anchor, two, three,
a hundred more tug
aimlessly under sail,
tacking from close-ups
of pleasure points
to interstices of private
littoral. Beneath veneers
of decay is grandeur
atop decline, like tin
under rust or lichen
on cedar that shelters
beams of pine hard
or soft with age invisible
to the once-invincible
family dining at the table below.

Any Big Question

The rain is knocking the mahogany
blossoms from the tall tree and drowning
out the thunderous pool pump on its way

to filling the streets and ending
this drought. Others know of other
things. I think each experience

of our existences is as worthwhile
as it isn't. I think the rain just stopped
and it did. I know the birds will begin

chirping again soon, and look, listen,
there they go, lusting after sustenance
and survival. It doesn't take answers

at the ready to ask any big question
just as inquisitiveness isn't required
to reveal the answers before you

aren't there, or are, or are lost, another
stainless screw in the pine needles
budgeted for and unworried over.

The annual seaside event brought families
of all races together under the trees to build
small crafts with volunteers, heedless

of advisories, before ceasing this year: all
you need to know of the concentration
of power and the allure of home.

When my team is at home, they bring light
to my nights. When they're away
it's as if life goes on without seeing

their slowly aging handsome faces.
I've come to learn a lot about confidence
and the importance of reaching out

for help with the things you love most
in order to perform better, love better,
by watching the man on the hill,

whose uniform is most lit
by the banks of bulbs showering light
from their height to his.

It's possible greed factors in,
or a negative quality is partner
to the competitive drive displayed,

but that's a baseball man's life,
an argument and difference of opinion
played out in confinement under rules

the skillful render flexible, his bones growing
suppler each day, forgetting what he'll learn
while the unreachable future grows dim

and the distant past is lustrous,
long enough, and likely lusty and
love-filled for a moment.

••

At the movies, it's the projector's beam
and each piece of dust that glows
before the shapes the screen reveals

to tell the story we've come for: a human story
making life a little more, therefore the opponent
world less; emotions lit up like signs

over exit doors, hands holding a partner's hand,
the street-lit nighttime stroll home to comfort,
some big dream, a tall sun's morning.

•••

Tonight the night depends on light
and its associated technologies: switch,
filament, oscillation, the glow

from glow-sticks wired to baits carried from sight
by lead to a depth of the fathomable sea,
and the one lobbed back from the bait's skating partner,

the balloon pinned at the surface of the drift,
roaming within limits. That's gravity –this swordfisherman's rig–
and free-from-gravity on display, differing densities,

a little temperature gradient, and a thin rubber membrane
desperate to burst and flaccidly follow tethering ounces
of lead down. The spreader's halogens, the instrument panel's

LCD glow, and the submerged fluorescent tube throwing waves
to make stars of plankton, hold us in a luminescent world
from which the radiant dome of our city can be seen; and the overhead stars

and planets, their clusters, sprays, apparent patterns, and bright blur.
To imagine what they're like beyond this strict perimeter of light
requires closed eyes, waiting, sleep, or a switch thrown to grow seer

like tonight's intended quarry: a toothless, nocturnal,
vampirish fish built to defeat its own hunger,
with saucer-sized eyes trained by ages at depth

to find the smallest specks of light, reflections of luckless
scales, mistakenly evolved opaque skins, insufficiently transparent
exoskeletons, with inky skin and a long serrated bill meant

to strafe and beat its prey literal inches away from functional death
followed by stars of dazzling individual brightness, agape at the calm
night's glassy sea-top's way of casting all from this middle, a precise self

grown another reflective and transparent surface, the water, the flying
fish's silhouetted stationary wings, the slowly burning meteor
that keeps falling until it becomes another airplane.

••••

The swordfish was hooked at the end of night after we fished
all night, the light just beginning to be guessed at to the east,
about 5:30 in middle June, longitude eighty-one-something.

It was dead when we hauled it over the transom into the daylight.
At the dock, we cut out its softball-sized eyes –all pupil, bound
in a bowl of bone– and passed them from hand to hand

before their rest on ice. Its body we sawed into steaks,
and our friends and families filled the evening air with grill-smoke
and the island chain was a sundown town, the world, and small again.

The Good Existence

Today's cool.
I can say it, winds
from the north
and gusty, though I've
said it before,
because it is.
Repetition
is how I live
as I go on living.

Teapot, watch, urchin
shell, and others:
all the words
I need this morning
are in my head,
or on the table,
or in the trees, like
this one: breeze,
which, I've prayed,
would push me along
the pressure ridge's edge
to a calmer day.

Soon I'll move
the things I've brought
to this summer's room
out and go
to work, and go
home and go
to work. Until then,
mahogany tree's

shade, bamboo's
click-clack and
rustle, porch with
rocking chair, repose,
repeating, living, gusts.

In The Light

The summer sun
throws it down,
soaking into streets
and built-up shores,
glancing off nearshore
waters given glinting colors,
an iris widened
by a pupil's shrinking in.

Schools of majua read
as green-gray cloud-shadows
or grass beds, shimmerless
until the net is hurled:
an encircling apparition,
projectile, trap, and tool.
In the light it flashes
and disappears
before it splashes,
tugged by a leaded perimeter
around the severed school's
frenzy of commensurate instincts:
chasing, sparkling, and all else
but sun and sea-bottom are shadow.

After a moment's rest,
the hem of the again-transparent
net is tugged inward, up
into its center, forcing flashings
from the majua's sides
as they lose the water it's lifted from,
glittering with shed scales.

Thousands of fish, a mirror
stripe on each translucent side,
a mirror head holding a big black eye,
are dumped into a basket
to drain and then into a cooler
where, when the boat rocks,
they flash and sparkle still.

This dumb chiaroscuro
pounds through sunglasses
until the gray, white, and
small blue coolers are full:
six hundred plus pounds
salted and iced, and salt
and ice give shape to light too.
The governance
of light renders words
unnecessary. Our words
might sparkle like that net
and disappear. They might flash,
but at the peril of thoughts
and afterthoughts, the doomed scintillas
their harness brought to bear.

Violets

Violets bloom in the spring-time, foreign season,
and in the summer it so often is. They're lovely
little flowers, found in a range of colors beside
violet, containing a ketone compound
called ionone which prevents the viewer
from smelling what she could smell
a moment ago, like a metaphor you'd never
make or see coming at you. Someday, this
lifetime of easy fame and meager fortunes
will be but more scentless water from the well
of Poncé de Leon, a tourist attraction of centuries-old
popularity, but until then the battle,
my hobby, if not my profession, rages on.

To Seaward

After the struggle,
I boarded my bicycle
and headed south
and southeast, which means
the beach, here and now,
and found my Hobie-Cat gone,
as I suspected.

It was a convenient arrangement
and then it was an object
at rest prone to staying
such so that I and it
donated a year untethered
to the wind and the manners
that long had held me.
Now, perhaps, we are in motion.

A new Wu-banger is in my ears,
big pilchards are stacked deep,
and a barracuda is tailing a snook.

My synapses have been rewired
to generate more joy along my surveys.
This little town is bursting
with opportunity, and some
among the earth's finest specimens
of human are here. The thin wall
which edges the coastal sidewalk,
now that it has been completed,
holds us in and protects us, and
at night, when the moon is bright,

guides us, too, and cannot but correct us
if to seaward we are wrong.

X-ray

I had my X-ray taken yesterday at the chiropractor's. It was strange, my sense of myself as aligned so utterly contradicted, in nearly real time, like a Polaroid. My spine shows considerable torque; lumbar vertebrae pinched on my left and gaping open on my right; the thoracic (where my problems lie) jammed together; most of my rib-heads out of what would be their comfortable resting-place. My intestines looked like the ghost of a full-bosomed woman with kinky hair, but Dr. Debbie said it looked like my digestive system was operating fine. Armed with this new information, she's going to try a fresh approach to my alignment. I'm going to rearrange my workspace, buy a new monitor and chair for the office, and refrain from self-adjusting my spine. She says I've made it hyper-mobile. Today, at her request, I did not go sailing. I went swimming, at Fort Zachary Taylor's beach, in clear water above a school of tarpon, after banking, before the post-office, shopping, bicycling. And now I have some hot sausages and rice to eat. Key West is a beautiful town they will succeed at one day in ruining. Even then, the bursts of frangipani blooms will be tough to beat.

About the Author

Arlo Haskell is a director of the Key West Literary Seminar, editor of the online journal *Littoral*, and publisher of Sand Paper Press. He lives with Ashley Kamen, his longtime companion, in Key West.

Also from Sand Paper Press

Stuart Krimko
The Sweetness of Herbert

Shawn Vandor
Fire at the End of the Rainbow